NEW YORK, 1965

malcolm X

SPEAKS OUT

Edited by

Nan Richardson,
Catherine Chermayeff
& Antoinette White

A Callaway  BoundSound Book™

Andrews and McMeel
A Universal Press Syndicate Company
Kansas City
1992

HARLEM, NEW YORK, 1963

I do not pretend to be a divine man, but I do believe in divine guidance, divine power, and in the fulfillment of divine prophecy. I am not educated nor am I an expert in any particular field. But I am sincere, and my sincerity is my credentials.

New York, March 12, 1964

DETROIT, C. 1952

I'm from America but I'm not an American. I didn't go there of my own free choice.... I come as one of the victims of America, one of the victims of Americanism, one of the victims of democracy, one of the victims of a very hypocritical system...representing itself as being qualified to tell people how to run their country when they can't get the dirty things that are going on in their own country straightened out.... Our people didn't go to America in the *Queen Mary*, we didn't go by

NEW YORK, 1963

Pan American, and we didn't go to America on the *Mayflower*. We went in slave ships, we went in chains. We weren't immigrants to America, we were cargo for purposes of a system that was bent upon making a profit. Now I am not here to condemn America, I am not here to make America look bad, but I am here to tell you the truth about the situation the black people in America find themselves confronted with. And if truth condemns America, then she stands condemned.

Ghana, May 13, 1964

WE LIVE IN ONE OF THE ROTTENEST COUNTRIES THAT HAS EVER EXISTED ON THIS EARTH. IT'S THE SYSTEM THAT IS ROTTEN; IT'S A POLITICAL AND ECONOMIC SYSTEM OF EXPLOITATION, OF OUTRIGHT HUMILIATION, DEGRADATION, DISCRIMINATION—ALL OF THE NEGATIVE THINGS THAT YOU CAN RUN INTO UNDER THIS SYSTEM THAT DISGUISES ITSELF AS A

DEMOCRACY.

New York, June 28, 1964

NEW YORK, 1963

Nineteen sixty-three started out in America with all the politicians talking about this being the hundredth year since the Emancipation Proclamation.

BIRMINGHAM, ALABAMA, 1963

They were going to celebrate "a century of progress in race relations." And then Martin Luther King went into Birmingham, Alabama, just trying to get a few Negroes to be able to sit down at a lunch counter and drink a cup of coffee. They ended up putting him in jail. They ended up putting thousands of Negroes in jail. And many of you saw on television how the police had those big vicious dogs, crushing the skulls of black people. They had water hoses turned on our women, stripping off the clothes from our own women, from our own children.... And it ended in the bombing of a church in Alabama where four little girls, Christians, sitting in Sunday school, singing about Jesus, were blown apart by people who claim to be Christians. And this happened in the year 1963. And the world saw this. The world saw what [it] had thought was going to be a year which would celebrate a hundred years of progress toward good race relations between white and black in the United States—and instead they saw one of the most inhuman, savage displays there in that country.

London, February 11, 1965

HARLEM, NEW YORK, 1968

The whole world thinks that America's race problem is being solved, when actually the masses of black people in America are still living in the ghettos or in the slums.

London, February 11, 1965

We are trapped in a vicious cycle of economic, intellectual, social, and political death. Inferior jobs, inferior housing, inferior education, which in turn again leads to inferior jobs. We spend a lifetime in this vicious circle...giving birth to children who see no hope or future but to follow in our miserable footsteps.

California, October 11, 1963

A MAN
OUR
PEOPLE
WERE
OUTRIGHT
SLAVES...

MEMPHIS, TENNESSEE, 1968

WE PULLED THE PLOWS LIKE HORSES. WE WERE BOUGHT AND SOLD FROM ONE PLANTATION TO ANOTHER LIKE YOU SELL CHICKENS OR LIKE YOU SELL A BAG OF POTATOES....GEORGE WASHINGTON EXCHANGED A BLACK MAN FOR A KEG OF MOLASSES....

ONE HUNDRED MILLION AFRICANS WERE UPROOTED FROM THE AFRICAN CONTINENT—WHERE ARE THEY TODAY?...THEIR BODIES ARE AT THE BOTTOM OF THE OCEAN, OR THEIR BLOOD AND THEIR BONES HAVE FERTILIZED THE SOIL OF THIS COUNTRY.

New York, April 8, 1964

IT WAS ONLY AFTER THE SPIRIT OF THE BLACK MAN WAS COMPLETELY BROKEN AND HIS DESIRE TO BE A MAN WAS COMPLETELY DESTROYED, THAT THEY TOOK THE PHYSICAL CHAINS FROM HIS ANKLES AND PUT THEM ON HIS MIND.

New York, July 5, 1964

HAVING COMPLETE CONTROL OVER AFRICA, THE COLONIAL POWERS OF EUROPE HAD PROJECTED THE IMAGE OF AFRICA NEGATIVELY...JUNGLE SAVAGES, CANNIBALS, NOTHING CIVILIZED....WE DIDN'T WANT ANYBODY TELLING US ANYTHING ABOUT AFRICA, MUCH LESS CALLING US AFRICANS. IN HATING AFRICA AND IN HATING THE AFRICANS, WE ENDED UP HATING OURSELVES....

WE HATED OUR HEADS, WE HATED THE SHAPE OF OUR NOSE....WE HATED THE COLOR OF OUR SKIN, HATED THE BLOOD OF AFRICA THAT WAS IN OUR VEINS.

WE DIDN'T HAVE CONFIDENCE IN ANOTHER BLACK MAN...WE DIDN'T THINK A BLACK MAN COULD DO ANYTHING EXCEPT PLAY SOME HORNS—. BUT IN SERIOUS THINGS, WHERE OUR FOOD, CLOTHING, SHELTER, AND EDUCATION WERE CONCERNED, WE TURNED TO THE MAN. WE NEVER THOUGHT IN TERMS OF BRINGING THESE THINGS INTO EXISTENCE FOR OURSELVES, BECAUSE WE FELT HELPLESS. WHAT MADE US FEEL HELPLESS WAS OUR HATRED FOR OURSELVES....

IT MADE US FEEL INFERIOR; IT MADE US FEEL INADEQUATE; MADE US FEEL HELPLESS. AND WHEN WE FELL VICTIMS TO THIS FEELING OF INADEQUACY OR INFERIORITY OR HELPLESSNESS, WE TURNED TO SOMEBODY ELSE TO SHOW US THE WAY.

Detroit, February 18, 1965

This is how you imprisoned us. Not just bringing us here and making us slaves. But the image that you created of our motherland and the image that you created of our people on that continent was a trap, was a prison, was a chain, was the worst form of slavery that has ever been invented by a so-called civilized race and a civilized nation since the beginning of the world.

Rochester, New York, February 16, 1965

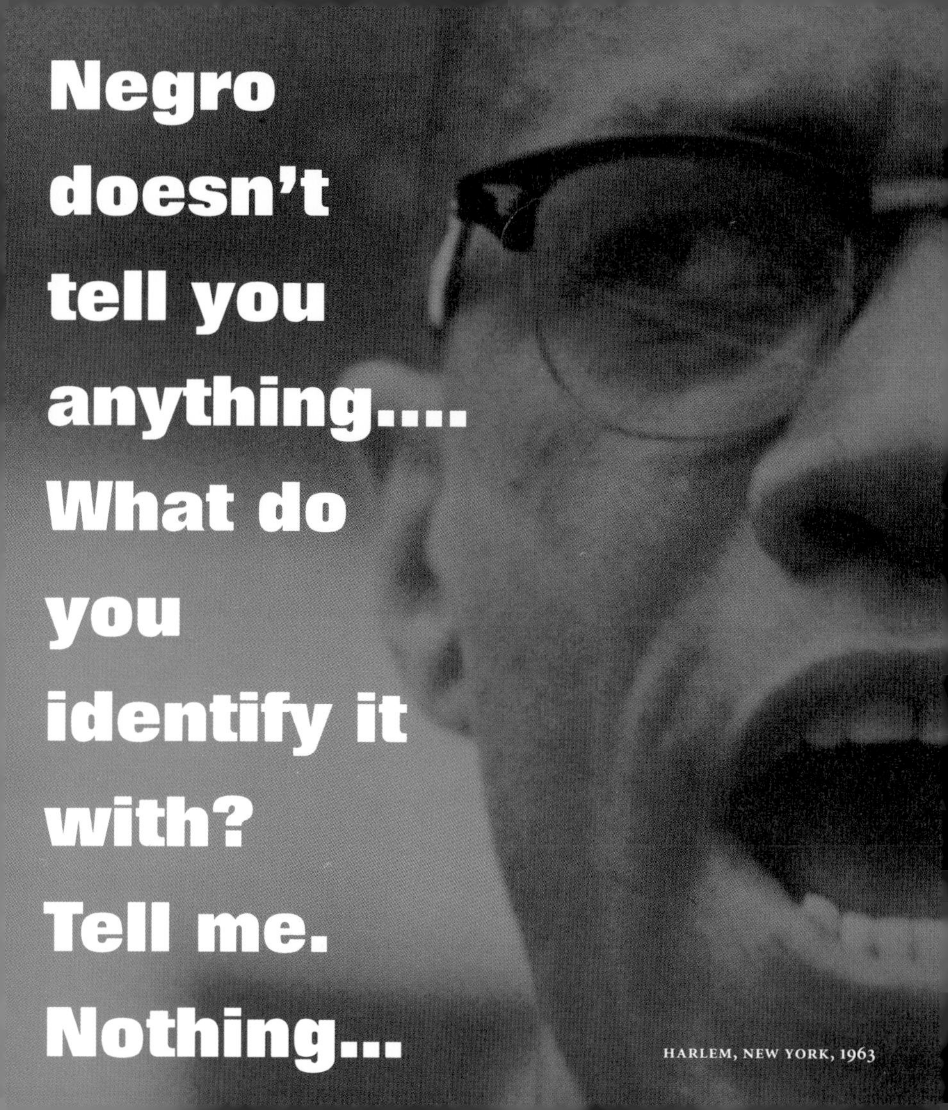

Negro doesn't tell you anything.... What do you identify it with? Tell me. Nothing...

HARLEM, NEW YORK, 1963

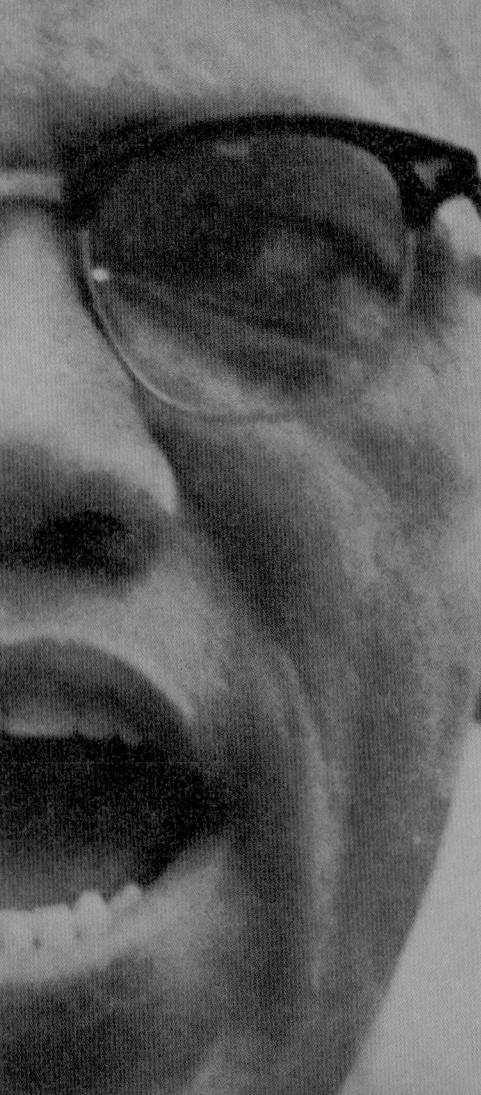

It doesn't give you a language, because there is no such thing as a Negro language. It doesn't give you a country, because there is no such thing as a Negro country. It doesn't give you a culture—there is no such thing as a Negro culture—it doesn't exist.

And this is the position that you and I are in here in America. Formerly we could be identified by the names we wore when we came here....But once our names were taken and our language was taken and our identity was destroyed and our roots were cut off with no history, we became like a stump, something dead.

New York, January 24, 1965

The limited education America has granted her ex-slaves has even already produced great unrest....

no man

with education equal to your own will serve you. The only way you can continue to rule us is with superior knowledge, by continuing to withhold equal education from our people. America has not given us equal education, but she has given us enough to make us want more and to make us demand equality of opportunity.

Cambridge, Massachusetts, March 24, 1961

ENGLEWOOD, NEW JERSEY, 1966

NEW YORK, 1965

We must stop drinking; we must stop smoking; we must stop committing fornication and adultery; we must stop gambling and cheating and using profanity; we must stop showing disrespect for our women; we must reform ourselves as parents so we can set the proper example for our children. Once we reform ourselves of these immoral habits, that makes us more godly, more godlike, more righteous. That means we are qualified, then, to be on God's side, and it puts God on our side. God becomes our champion.

Interview with Kenneth Clark, June 1963

NEW YORK, C. 1963

Why do we, black people, turn to Islam. The religion that many of our forefathers practiced before we were kidnapped and brought into this country by the American white man was the religion of Islam.

This has been destroyed in textbooks of the American educational system to try and make it appear that we were nothing but animals or savages before we were brought here. But when you go back, you'll find that there were large Muslim empires that stretched all the way down into equatorial Africa, the Mali Empire, Guinea. All these places—their religion was Islam.

New York, April 8, 1964

One of the things that made the Black Muslim movement grow was its emphasis upon things African. African blood, African origin, African culture, African ties...we discovered that deep within the subconscious of the black man in this country, he is still more African than he's American.

Detroit, February 18, 1965

NEW YORK, 1963

The Black Muslim movement's... contribution to the black struggle for freedom in this country was militancy. It made many of our people dare to get loud for the first time in 400 years.

New York, January 7, 1965

Muslims are not a hate group. We're not bitter toward the white man; in fact, I believe that we Muslims who follow Mr. Elijah Mohammed get along better with white people than Christian Negroes...who profess to love white people.... They recognize us Muslims and respect us for what we are just as we respect them....They don't have any trouble out of us; we don't have any trouble out of them.

Interview with William Kunstler, March 1960

MECCA, 1964

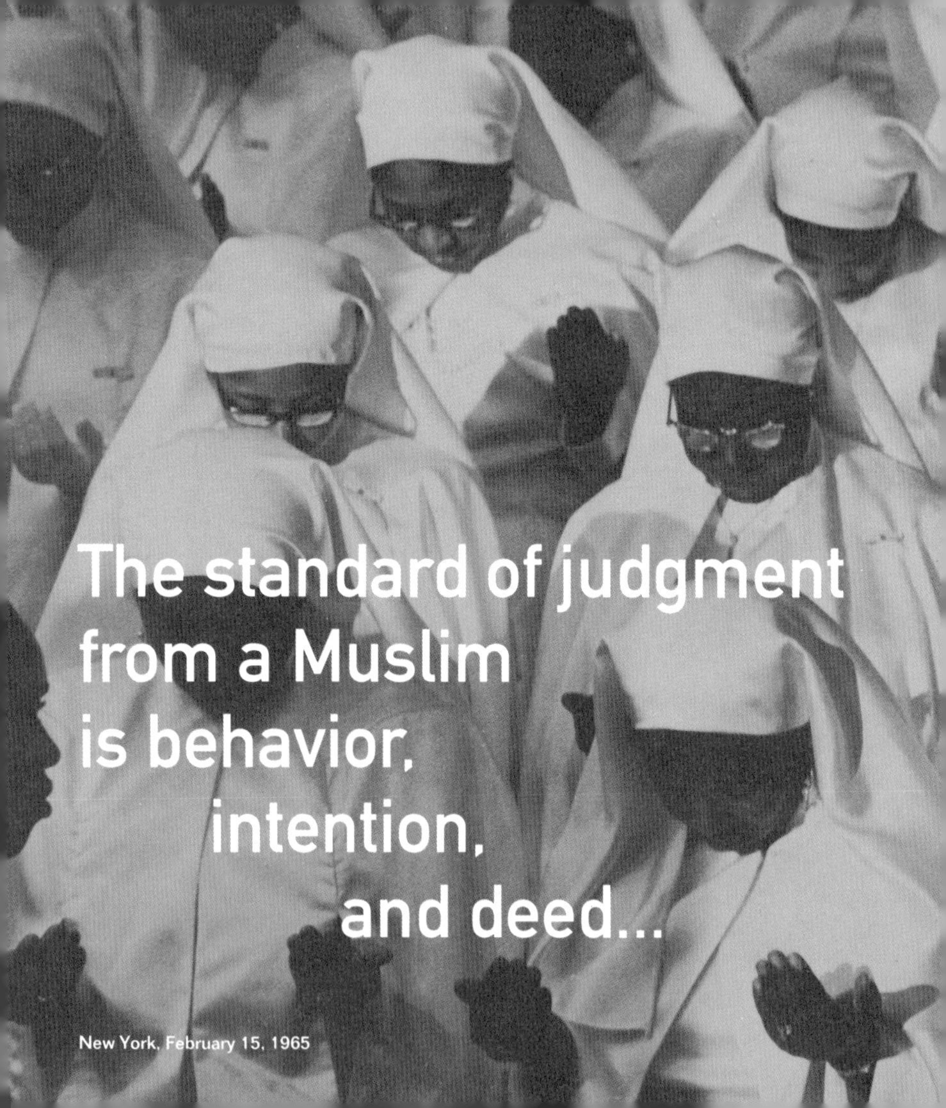

The standard of judgment from a Muslim is behavior,

intention,

and deed...

New York, February 15, 1965

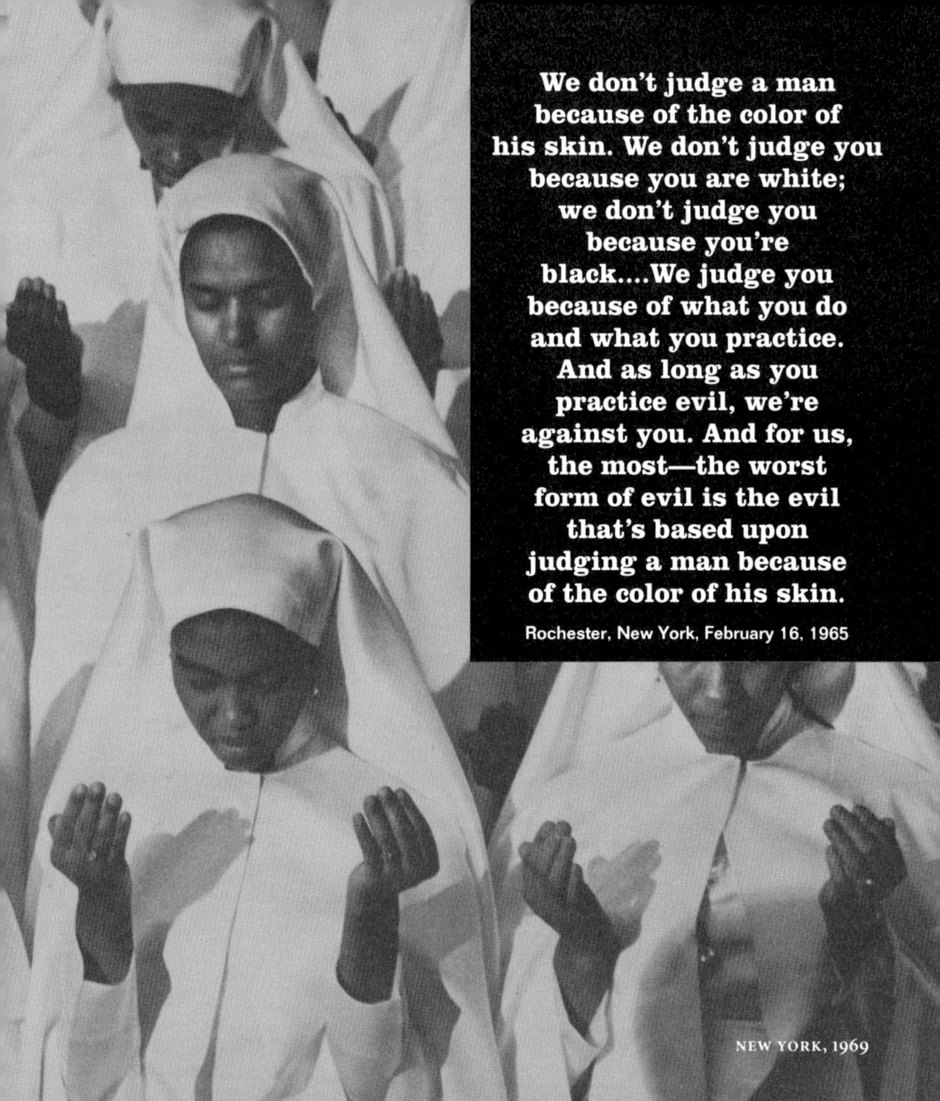

We don't judge a man because of the color of his skin. We don't judge you because you are white; we don't judge you because you're black....We judge you because of what you do and what you practice. And as long as you practice evil, we're against you. And for us, the most—the worst form of evil is the evil that's based upon judging a man because of the color of his skin.

Rochester, New York, February 16, 1965

NEW YORK, 1969

HARLEM, NEW YORK, 1965

I believe in recognizing every human being as a human being, neither white, black, brown, nor red. When you are dealing with humanity as one family, there's no question of integration or intermarriage. It's just one human being marrying another human being or one human being living with another human being.

I may say, though, that I don't think the burden to defend any such position should ever be put upon the black man. Because it is the white man collectively who has shown that he is hostile towards integration and towards intermarriage and towards other strides towards oneness.

Interview with Pierre Berton, January 1965

All of our people have the same goals. The same objective. That objective is freedom, justice, equality. All of us want recognition and respect as human beings. We don't want to be integrationists. Nor do we want to be separationists. We want to be human beings.

New York, April 8, 1964

NORTH CAROLINA, 1950

Segregation is that which is forced upon inferiors by superiors. Separation is done voluntarily by two equals....We are against segregation because it is unjust and we are against integration because its hypothesis is a false solution to a real problem.

WUST Interview, May 1963

The Supreme Court decision has never been enforced. Desegregation has never taken place. The promises have never been fulfilled. We have received only tokens, substitutes, trickery, and deceit.

Interview with Alex Haley, May 1963

America is worse than South Africa, because not only is America racist, but she also is deceitful and hypocritical. South Africa preaches segregation and practices segregation. She, at least, practices what she preaches. America preaches integration and practices segregation. She preaches one thing while deceitfully practicing another.

Cairo, Egypt, July 17, 1964

NEW YORK, 1962

If we are
we're
of it. In fact,
that our people
extreme and an
cannot be
a moderate

extremists not ashamed the conditions suffer are extreme illness cured with medicine.

Paris, November 23, 1964

USE OF CO
PROPER
BOO
2.00
AFRICANS
RECRUITING
HIST

HARLEM, NEW YORK, 1963

It's time for you and me now to let the world know how peaceful we are, how well-meaning we are, how law-abiding we wish to be. But at the same time we have to let the world know we'll blow their world sky-high if we're not respected and recognized and treated the same as other human beings.

New York, July 5, 1964

HARLEM, NEW YORK, C. 1961

Don't let anybody tell you anything about the odds against you. If they draft you, they send you to Korea and make you face 800 million Chinese.

NEW YORK, C. 1962

If you can be brave over there, you can be brave right here.... If you fight here, you will at least know what you're fighting for.

Cleveland, April 3, 1964

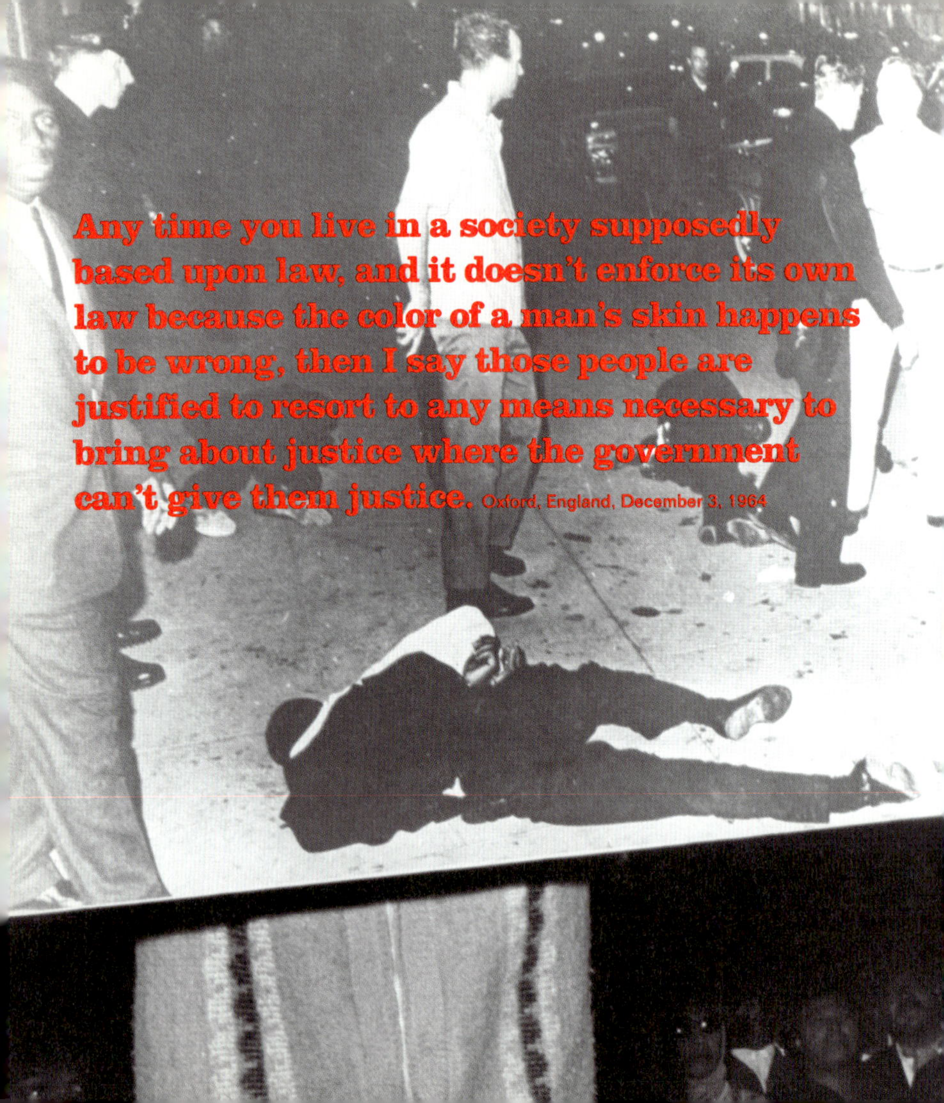

Any time you live in a society supposedly based upon law, and it doesn't enforce its own law because the color of a man's skin happens to be wrong, then I say those people are justified to resort to any means necessary to bring about justice where the government can't give them justice. Oxford, England, December 3, 1964

HARLEM, NEW YORK, 1963

The only people in this country who are asked to be nonviolent are black people. I've never heard anybody go to the Ku Klux Klan and teach them nonviolence, or to the [John] Birch Society. I believe we should protect ourselves by any means necessary when attacked by racists.

London, February 11, 1965

IN AREAS WHERE OUR PEOPLE ARE CONSTANT VICTIMS OF BRUTALITY...WE SHOULD...DEFEND OUR LIVES AND OUR PROPERTY IN TIMES OF EMERGENCY....WHEN OUR PEOPLE ARE BEING BITTEN BY DOGS, THEY ARE WITHIN THEIR RIGHTS TO KILL THOSE DOGS.

WE SHOULD BE PEACEFUL, LAW-ABIDING—BUT THE TIME HAS COME FOR THE AMERICAN NEGRO TO FIGHT BACK IN SELF-DEFENSE WHENEVER AND WHEREVER HE IS BEING UNJUSTLY OR UNLAWFULLY ATTACKED.

IF THE GOVERNMENT THINKS I AM WRONG FOR SAYING THIS, THEN LET THE GOVERNMENT START DOING ITS JOB.

New York, March 12, 1964

SALISBURY, NORTH CAROLINA, C. 1964

I RES
GOVER
AND RE
LAW.

GOVERNMENT

RESPECT

PECT

NMENT

SPECT

BUT DOES THE

AND THE LAW

US?

New York, December 27, 1964

CHICAGO, 1962

LAST SUMMER... THE BLACKS WERE RIOTING—RIOTS, ACTUALLY [THAT] WEREN'T RIOTS IN THE FIRST PLACE; THEY WERE REACTIONS AGAINST POLICE BRUTALITY....

HARLEM, NEW YORK, 1965

WHEN THE STORE WINDOWS WERE BROKEN IN THE BLACK COMMUNITY, IMMEDIATELY IT WAS MADE TO APPEAR THAT THIS WAS BEING DONE NOT BY THE PEOPLE WHO WERE REACTING OVER CIVIL RIGHTS VIOLATIONS, [BUT BY] HOODLUMS, VAGRANTS, CRIMINALS, WHO WANTED NOTHING OTHER THAN TO GET INTO THE STORES AND TAKE THE MERCHANDISE. BUT THIS IS WRONG. IN AMERICA THE BLACK COMMUNITY IN WHICH WE LIVE IS NOT OWNED BY US. THE LANDLORD IS WHITE. THE MERCHANT IS WHITE. IN FACT, THE ENTIRE ECONOMY OF THE BLACK COMMUNITY IS CONTROLLED BY SOMEONE WHO

DOESN'T EVEN LIVE THERE. THE STORE THAT WE TRADE WITH IS OPERATED BY SOMEONE ELSE AND THESE ARE THE PEOPLE WHO SUCK THE ECONOMIC BLOOD OF OUR COMMUNITY....THEY CONTROL THE RADIO PROGRAMS THAT CATER TO US; THEY CONTROL THE NEWSPAPERS, THE ADVERTISING. THEY CONTROL OUR MINDS. AND WHEN YOU SEE THE BLACKS REACT, ...YOU GET THE IMPRESSION THAT BECAUSE THEY ARE DESTROYING WHERE THEY LIVE, THAT THEY ARE DESTROYING THEIR OWN PROPERTY. NO. THEY CAN'T GET TO THE MAN, SO THEY GET AT WHAT HE OWNS.

London, February 11, 1965

NEW YORK, 1963

IF VIOLENCE IS WRONG IN AMERICA, VIOLENCE IS WRONG ABROAD. IF IT IS WRONG TO BE VIOLENT DEFENDING BLACK WOMEN AND BLACK CHILDREN AND BLACK BABIES AND BLACK MEN, THEN IT IS WRONG FOR AMERICA TO DRAFT US AND MAKE US VIOLENT ABROAD IN DEFENSE OF HER. AND IF IT IS RIGHT FOR AMERICA TO DRAFT US, AND TEACH US HOW TO BE VIOLENT IN DEFENSE OF HER, THEN IT IS RIGHT FOR YOU AND ME TO DO WHATEVER IS NECESSARY TO DEFEND OUR OWN PEOPLE RIGHT HERE IN THIS COUNTRY.

Detroit, November 10, 1963

HARLEM, NEW YORK, 1963

THE RACIAL SPARKS IGNITED HERE IN AMERICA TODAY COULD EASILY TURN INTO A FLAMING FIRE ABROAD...COULD ENGULF ALL THE PEOPLE OF THIS EARTH INTO A GIANT RACE WAR.

THE DARK MASSES OF AFRICA AND ASIA AND LATIN AMERICA ARE ALREADY SEETHING WITH BITTERNESS, ANIMOSITY, HOSTILITY, UNREST, AND IMPATIENCE WITH THE RACIAL INTOLERANCE THAT THEY THEMSELVES HAVE EXPERIENCED AT THE HANDS OF THE WHITE WEST.

New York, April 8, 1964

A devil is still a devil whether he wears a bed sheet or a Brooks Brothers suit.

Interview with Alex Haley, May 1963

HARLEM, NEW YORK, 1963

I'M NOT BLANKETLY CONDEMNING ALL WHITES. ALL OF THEM DON'T OPPRESS. ALL OF THEM AREN'T IN A POSITION TO. BUT MOST OF THEM ARE, AND MOST OF THEM DO.

New York, November 29, 1964

[Furthermore, since the Bible] promises that non-Christians will be destroyed in a fiery death someday by God himself, I find it difficult that Catholics and Christians accuse us of teaching racial supremacy or racial hatred, because their own history and their own teachings are filled with it.

Interview with William Kunstler, March 1960

Revolution is like a forest fire. It burns everything in its path.

New York, March 19, 1964

This is a real revolution. Revolution is always based on land. Revolution is never based on begging somebody for an integrated cup of coffee. Revolutions are never fought by turning the other cheek. Revolutions are never based upon love your enemy and pray for those who spitefully use you. And revolutions are never waged singing, "We Shall Overcome." Revolutions are based upon bloodshed. Revolutions are never compromising. Revolutions are never based upon negotiations. Revolutions are never based upon any kind of tokenism whatsoever....Revolutions overturn systems, and there is no system on this earth which has proven itself more corrupt, more criminal, than this system that in 1964 still colonizes twenty-two million African-Americans.

New York, April 8, 1964

SELMA, ALABAMA, 1965

You don't have to criticize Reverend Martin Luther King, Jr. His actions criticize him....

Any Negro who teaches other Negroes to turn the other cheek in the face of attack is disarming that Negro of his God-given right, of his moral right, of his natural right, of his intelligent right to defend himself. Everything in nature can defend itself, and is right in defending itself, except the American Negro. And men like King...he doesn't tell them, "Don't fight each other." "Don't fight the white man" is what he's saying in essence, because the followers of Martin Luther King, Jr. will cut each other from head to foot, but they will not do anything to defend themselves against the attacks of the white man....

White people follow King. White people pay King. White people subsidize King. White people support King. But the masses of black people don't support Martin Luther King, Jr. King is the best weapon that the white man, who wants to brutalize Negroes, has ever gotten in this country, because he is setting up a situation where, when the white man wants to attack Negroes, they can't defend themselves.

Interview with Kenneth Clark, June 1963

Dr. King wants the same thing I want—freedom. Now his method of going about getting it is the nonviolent way. We may differ in method, but that does not mean we differ in objective.

Panel with Louis Lomax, April 1964

WASHINGTON, D.C., 1964

The political philosophy of black nationalism means that the black man should control the politics and the politicians in his own community....The economic philosophy of black nationalism is pure and simple. It only means that we should control the economy of our community....The social philosophy of black nationalism only means that we have to get together and remove the evils, the vices, alcoholism, drug addiction, and other evils that are destroying the moral fiber of our community....

We've got to change our own minds about each other. We have to see each other with new eyes. We have to see each other as brothers and sisters. We have to come together with warmth so we can develop [the] unity and harmony that's necessary to get this problem solved ourselves....

It'll be the ballot or the bullet. It'll be liberty or it'll be death.

Cleveland, April 3, 1964

HARLEM, NEW YORK, 1968

NO PARKING
1 HOUR PARKING
COME
TO THE
OTIC GANGSTERS

HARLEM, NEW YORK, 1963

SELMA, ALABAMA, 1965

How can we get political power? We have to organize the people of Harlem in a door-by-door campaign, I mean door by door, house by house, people by people, person by person, and you have to make them feel so ashamed that they're not registered they won't even come out of the house. We have to create an atmosphere in Harlem— and when I say Harlem, the greater New York area—in which every black man will feel like he's a traitor if he's not a registered voter. His ballot will be like a bullet.

New York, July 5, 1964

MISSISSIPPI, 1963

Once we can get our people actively engaged in politics, we feel that we will then be in a better position to bring pressure on the politicians who now exploit our people and perpetuate conditions of poverty and slums and vice and other forms of crime.

New York, July 4, 1964

We are actually fighting for rights that are even greater than civil rights and that is human rights.

New York, April 8, 1964

SELMA TO MONTGOMERY, ALABAMA, 1965

I BELIEVE THAT IT IS POSSIBLE
FOR BROTHERHOOD
TO BE BROUGHT
ABOUT AMONG ALL PEOPLE,
BUT I DON'T DELUDE
MYSELF INTO
DREAMING OR FALLING
FOR A DREAM
THAT THIS EXISTS BEFORE IT EXISTS....
SOME OF THE
LEADERS OF OUR PEOPLE
IN THIS COUNTRY...SAY...THEY
BELIEVE IN
THIS DREAM. BUT WHILE
THEY'RE DREAMING,
OUR PEOPLE
ARE HAVING
A NIGHTMARE.

Interview with Les Crane, December 27, 1964

WASHINGTON, D.C., 1963

I'm no stranger to danger. I have lived with danger all my life. I never expect to die of old age. I know that I have done the very best that I could for our people....As I told you when we first began, after I was expelled from the Black Muslims, I did not want an organization that depended on the life of one man. The organization must be able to survive on its own.

MALCOLM X OUTSIDE HIS HOUSE
THE MORNING AFTER IT WAS FIREBOMBED,
ONE WEEK BEFORE HIS DEATH, 1965

I
live as if
I am
already
dead.

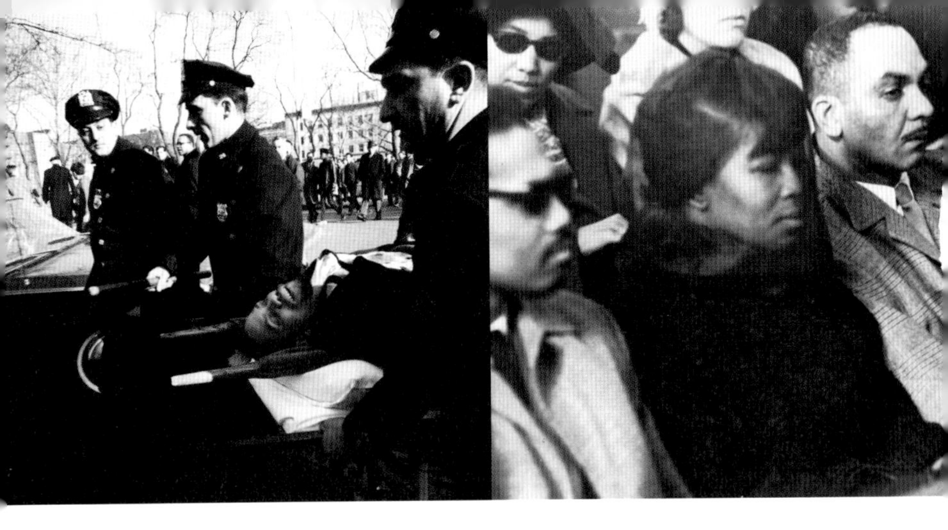

NEW YORK, 1965

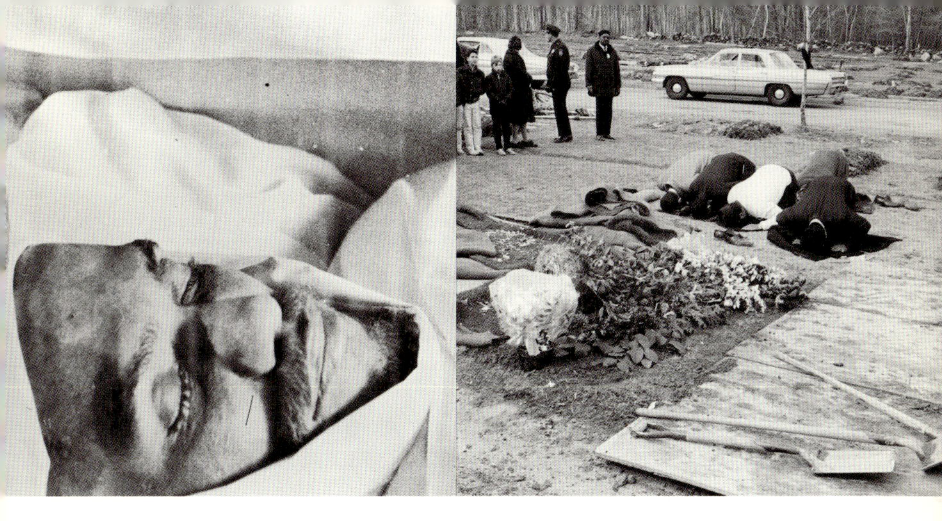

NEW YORK, 1965

LANSING, C. 1934

BOSTON, 1939

BOSTON, 1939

BOSTON, 1939

CHRONOLOGY

1925 Born on May 19th in Omaha, Nebraska. He is the fourth of the Reverend Earl and Louise Little's eight children.

1929 Ku Klux Klan sets fire to the Little house. Family moves to East Lansing, Michigan.

1931 Malcolm X's father, a Baptist minister and militant separatist, is beaten to death, allegedly by white supremacists.

1938 Expelled from school and placed in a juvenile detention center in Mason, Michigan. Its directors, however, soon enroll him in the local junior high school where he is elected president and rises to third in his class.

1940 Moves to Boston and finds work as a shoeshine boy and soda jerk.

1941 Moves to Harlem. Is fired from his job as a sandwich seller on a railroad lounge car for using marijuana and alcohol. Works as a waiter at Small's Paradise, a nightclub favored by the Harlem underworld, but is fired for pimping.

1942 Becomes a street hustler in New York.

1943 Judged psychologically unfit (4F) for military service after threatening to incite black revolts at army bases.

1944 Begins burglary ring in Boston.

1945 Arrested for possession of a stolen watch.

1946 Starts ten-year term for robbery.

1947 Begins to educate himself in jail by reading Latin, philosophy, science, history, archeology, linguistics and copying the dictionary word for word.

1948 Transferred to Norfolk prison (an experimental facility without bars and with a large library).

1949 Begins correspondence with Elijah Mohammed; converts to Islam and changes his name to Malcolm X.

1950 Writes to friends and to government officials about Islam and racial injustice.

1952 Paroled from prison.

1953 Moves to Detroit and in three months triples membership of its Nation of Islam Temple by "fishing" for converts in bars and in pool halls. Organizes his first temple in Boston, Massachusetts. Works for Ford Motor Company.

1954 Appointed minister for the Nation of Islam's Harlem Temple. Preaches seven times a week and conducts nightly adult education courses.

1955 Opens Temple 15 in Atlanta.

1956 Meets Betty X, a nurse and teacher at the Nation's Harlem Temple.

1957 Forms two dozen congregations nationwide and founds the newspaper, ***Mohammed Speaks***.

1958 Marries Betty. Attilah, the first of their six daughters, is born. They live in East Elmhurst, Queens.

1959 Visits Egypt, Saudi Arabia, Sudan, Nigeria, Ghana.

1961 Elijah Mohammed retires to Arizona for health reasons. Malcolm X assumes his public duties.

1962 Appointed national minister for the Nation of Islam.

1963 "The chickens (have) come home to roost," says Malcolm of JFK's assassination—and is subsequently silenced for thirty days by the Nation.

1964 Makes his first pilgrimage to Mecca. Takes the Islamic name El-hajj Malik El-Shabazz. Delivers the first of the seminal "The Ballot or the Bullet" speeches in Cleveland. Confronts Elijah Mohammad about his alleged adultery, breaks with Nation of Islam and founds both the Muslim Mosque, Inc. and the Organization of Afro-American Unity. Embarks on five-month speaking tour of Africa. Meets with heads of state of Egypt, Kenya, Uganda, Ghana, Tanzania, and Guinea. At University of Ghana delivers speech on "The Plight of 22 Million Afro-Americans in the United States."

1965 His home is firebombed (no one is injured). A week later, on February 21st, he is gunned down and fatally wounded by three assassins while speaking at the Audubon Ballroom in Harlem.

NEW YORK, 1964

WASHINGTON, D.C., 1963

NEW YORK, 1964

MIAMI, 1964

HISTORY IS A PEOPLE'S MEMORY.

New York, June 28, 1964

SO WHEN YOU SELECT HEROES ABOUT WHICH BLACK CHILDREN OUGHT TO BE TAUGHT, LET THEM BE BLACK HEROES WHO HAVE DIED FIGHTING FOR THE BENEFIT OF BLACK PEOPLE. THEY DON'T TEACH US THAT BUT THIS IS THE KIND OF HISTORY WE WANT TO LEARN...

Paris, November 23, 1964

NEW YORK, 1965

PHOTOGRAPHY CREDITS

O'Neal L. Abel, 6-7; Bob Adelman/Magnum Photos Inc., 1,27, 91 (second from top); AP/Wide World Photos, 13; (Chicago 1961) Eve Arnold/Magnum Photos Inc., 5; Bruce Davidson/Magnum Photos Inc., 17, 42-43, 78-79, 82-83; Elliott Erwitt/Magnum Photos Inc., 40-41; Leonard Freed/ Magnum Photos Inc., 38; Charles Gatewood/Magnum Photos Inc., 74-75; Burt Glinn/Magnum Photos Inc., 61; Robert L. Haggins, 30, 32-33, 46-47, 48-49, 50-51, 66, 76-77, 91 (third from top, bottom); Lawrence Henry, Schomburg Center for Research in Black Culture, The New York Public Library, 2-3, 28, 93; James Karales, 70-71; John Launois/Black Star, 35, 91 (top); Danny Lyon/Magnum Photos Inc., 58-59; Roger Malloch/Magnum Photos Inc., 36-37; Charles Moore/Black Star, 14-15, 55, 80; Ted Russell, Life Magazine/Time Warner Inc., 23, 24; Schomburg Center for Research in Black Culture, The New York Public Library, 9, 88 (right), 89 (left), 90 (top through bottom); UPI/ Bettmann Archive, cover, 18-19, 52-53, 64, 68, 73, 86-87, 88 (left), 89 (right), back cover; Fred Ward/Black Star, 85.

TEXT CREDITS

All text copyright Betty Shabazz and Pathfinder Press, reprinted by permission, with the exception of the following:

p. 87, from *The Autobiography of Malcolm X* with the assistance of Alex Haley, copyright ©1965 Alex Haley and Betty Shabazz (Ballantine Books, 1973). Reprinted by permission; pp. 29 and 72, from *The Negro Protest* by Kenneth Clark (Beacon Press, 1955). Reprinted by permission; pp. 42 and 68 from *Playboy Magazine*, May 1963. Reprinted by permission of Playboy Enterprises; p. 86 Malcolm X as remembered by Earl Grant, in *Malcolm A to X*, compiled by David Gallen (Carroll & Graf, 1992). Reprinted by permission of the publisher.

Charles Melcher and Nicholas Callaway, Producers

Nan Richardson and Catherine Chermayeff, Project Editors, Umbra Editions, Inc.

Antoinette White, Editor • Thomas West, Audio Editor • True Sims, Production Manager

Reiner Design Consultants, Inc., Book & Jacket Design

Eulalia Herrero Salas, Associate Editor, Umbra Editions, Inc.

Ivan Wong, Toshiya Masuda, Production Associates

Martha Lazar, Editorial Assistant • Meredith Ward, Copy Editor

Our thanks to the following individuals who assisted and advised us:
May Castleberry, Whitney Museum • Glenn Thompson, Writers and Readers • Lucy Fisher, Warner Bros. • Andy Karsch, Longfellow Pictures • Jonathan David, Tulip Films • Louise Neri, Parkett • Karen Kelly, DIA • Eithne Richardson • Donna Fox, PBS • Bob Schwartz, Pathfinder • Bill Thomas, Lucinda Wong, Mark Torres, and Pam Burton, Pacifica Radio • Julie Simms, Bettmann Archives • David Strettell, Mary Ann Price, Matthew Antezzo, Magnum • Robert Haggins • Doris Fong, Life Picture Service • Flip Schulke

First Edition

Library of Congress Cataloging-in-Publication Data
X, Malcolm, 1925 – 1965
Malcolm X Speaks Out/Edited by Nan Richardson,
Catherine Chermayeff, Antoinette White
p. cm.
1. X, Malcolm, 1925 – 1965—Quotations. 2. United States—Race relations—Quotations, maxims, etc.
I. Richardson, Nan. II. Chermayeff, Catherine III. White, Antoinette.
BP223.Z8L5795 1992
320.5 4—dc20 92-32771
CIP
ISBN 0-8362-8011-3; $17.95 (with CD)
ISBN 0-8362-8010-5; $9.95

Front and back of jacket photograph: UPI/Bettmann Archive

Back cover and front flap: Courtesy: Ossie Davis. Reprinted by permission.